Poems for Teens

Poems for Teens

Francis Emson Dakwa

Strategic Book Publishing and Rights Co.

Copyright © 2015 Francis Emson Dakwa. All rights reserved.

No part of this book may be reproduced or transmitted in any form or by any means, graphic, electronic, or mechanical, including photocopying, recording, taping, or by any information storage retrieval system, without the permission, in writing, of the publisher. For more information, send a letter to our Houston, TX, address, Attention Subsidiary Rights Department, or e-mail: support@sbpra.net.

Strategic Book Publishing and Rights Co.
12620 FM 1960, Suite A4-507
Houston, TX 77065
www.sbpra.com

For information about special discounts for bulk purchases, please contact Strategic Book Publishing and Rights Co. Special Sales at bookorder@sbpra.net.

ISBN: 978-1-63135-382-6

Dedicated to Silas Tatenda

Contents

Preface	xi

OUR HAPPINESS — 1

We Are the Happy Teens	3
Let Youngsters Enjoy Life	4
We Want to Wriggle	5
My Regalia, Leave Me Alone	6
I Shall Fall in Love	7
Are You My Only Boy?	8
The Gospel Wave	9
When I Become a Man	10
As I Become a Woman	11
I Want to Play Tennis	12

OUR NEEDS — 13

Give Me That Happiness	15
I Need a Home, Dad	16
Understand Me, Dear Mum	17
Companions of My Age	18
Food Is Gone, Alas!	19

Keep Me Company, Dear Friends	20
I Want to Be Loved	22
Oh, Lord! Let Me Sing	23
Down the Straight Lane	24
Who Hears My Call?	26

ON HIV AND AIDS — 27

Stop the Deadly Virus	29
I Am Sick, Mum; Support Me	30
Whose Fault Is It?	31
Wait in Patience	32
Lonely, Lonely Am I	33
Is It My Fault?	34
My Faith	35
What Caused My Sickness?	36
Prevention, Prevention	37
I'm Dying, Mum	38

OUR PROBLEMS — 39

We Are the Teens	41
I Am Confused	42
A Girl Calls	43
I Am a Boy	44
As Teens Look Round	45
Let Me Discover	46
The Young Criminal	47

Parents, Nurture Your Children	48
Question Concerning God	49
Time to Crave, Time to Achieve	50

OUR VIEWS — 51

Do Not Taunt Me	53
I Can Never Be You	54
I Choose to Wander Alone	55
The Teens Are Here	56
I Come Home, There Is No Mum	57
Hey, Boy, Stop There	58
Hop, Step, Jump	59
Detective Inspector Hangman	60
Friend of the Teens	61
Show Me Myself	62

Preface

Poems for Teens is an anthology of fifty poems dedicated to children in their teens. These poems are subdivided into five themes: *Our Happiness*, *Our Needs*, *On HIV and AIDS*, *Our Problems*, and *Our Views*. Adolescence is depicted as a period of challenge and transition when children graduate from childhood to adulthood. The youngsters appeal to us to understand them as they set out to develop an identity for themselves and crave autonomy. As we read through these poems, let us join the teens in their turbulent experiences and guide them to success.

—F. E. D.

OUR HAPPINESS

We Are the Happy Teens

We are the happy teens.
Do not think us crazy,
We are not all lazy,
But we enjoy life as queens.

We are the active teens,
Who should not be sloppy.
We are nobody's carbon copy,
As plump as garden beans.

We are the majestic teens,
Not bothered about anyone else,
Towering with our blue jeans,
Breathing the air so fresh.

We are the growing teens,
So tender, yet so young,
In that world of dreams,
As our birthdays are sung.

Let Youngsters Enjoy Life

Let youngsters enjoy life.
It is their time.
Should they not sprout
Like that kettle spout?

A joy to watch,
Youngsters must not scratch,
Sky is the limit,
Your dreams don't quit.

We used to be
Youngsters, tender like you.
Take courage and see,
The fulfillment that's true.

Be happy as ever,
Your friendships don't sever.
They bring the comfort,
You need the fort.

We Want to Wriggle

We want to wriggle
Like the maggots around.
Enjoying the reggae music
And the rhumba dance.

What of the rock 'n roll?
We roll and roll,
Turning topsy and turvy.
Join us in the fun.

We rep and talk
The love from within,
Blowing these roofs apart,
Exciting moments for us.

Our song fills the air,
Lifting hands and heads,
Jumping to free ourselves
As we enjoy that beat.

My Regalia, Leave Me Alone

My regalia, leave me alone.
Why bother about what I put on?
Is it any of your business
That I must put on whatever?
What pleases me, let me have.

I love that spaghetti-strap top;
It makes me feel like myself.
When the air so fresh surrounds,
And blows my hair up and down,
I shall be free to enjoy the world.

Girls cannot be like grannies,
But faded jeans are here to stay.
We shall not be criticized, rebuked.
What's wrong with what we love?
Do not dictate to us, dear mums.

Sometimes there is no difference,
Betwixt the girl and her mum.
I wear what you also wear.
The dad, the sons are one;
We both put on the fancies.

I Shall Fall in Love

I shall fall in love
With whom I really choose.
The beautiful girl I saw
The other day in town,
How you attracted me.
Only the heavens can tell!

I shall not ask you
Where you came from, dear.
I don't care who's your mum,
Nor why you don't have a dad.
I love you as you are.

Your eyes, your eyelids there,
Called me to draw so near.
When I beheld those lashes
And cheeks painted so red,
I thought I saw an angel!

Are You My Only Boy?

Are you my only boy,
Who whispered love to me?
I am not that toy
You think me to be.

Yes, I chose you alone,
The only one I know.
Our true love must grow.
You are my precious stone.

I can't imagine a life
Walked and shared without you.
Love penetrates like a knife,
Appetizing as sweet-smelling stew.

Faithful we shall walk together,
Until the day of our wedding.
Tears of sorrow shall fly away,
As we blend together like bee and honey.

The Gospel Wave

The Gospel wave has come,
To give joy to the soul
And shape the lives of teens,
Seeking and searching round
For that precious possession.

The songs of the Saviour
Echo in the ears of youths,
To bring life where there is none
And pour happiness to the heart.
Give us, now, the Gospel rhythms.

The sounds of guitars harmonise
And bring together all the youngsters,
Bonded together in the Master's wings
Like doves seeking a haven of rest.
Please, join the tune that vibrates.

I shall not miss those singers
As they chorus tunes of heaven
That bring solace to the troubled heart.
Listen, take part, and dance.
Chew and swallow those vibrations.

When I Become a Man

When I become a man,
I shall marry a woman,
The most beautiful and tall,
Towering above the wall.

When I become a man,
I shall work as hard
To buy myself that car
And show it to Stan.

When I become a man,
I shall buy myself a house,
Having sold all the cows,
And live there with sweet Shaun.

When I become a man,
I shall board a plane
And travel with my Shaun,
Enjoying our lives without shame.

As I Become a Woman

As I become a woman,
Let me groom my person
To be the shining star,
A model for all time.

I shall tend my beauty,
And care for my looks,
And mould my figure.
That makes me a woman.

I shall cherish my freedom
And buy myself a flat,
Live as cosy as ever,
Breathing the air so fresh.

I Want to Play Tennis

I want to play tennis,
Like that tennis star
Who reached great heights
And gained the world!

I want to play soccer,
And dribble the ball
That brought such fame
To the players bygone.

I want to play golf,
Criss-crossing the plain.
I love the white ball
That leads to the riches.

I want to play chess
And be like a thinker,
Who shall solve all problems.
Let me conquer the world.

OUR NEEDS

Give Me That Happiness

Give me that happiness
I need in life,
And remove the uneasiness,
The life of strife.

I want the joy
I had as a boy.
Where did it go,
To leave me low?

Mum, Dad, bring love.
I long for peace.
Like that sweet dove,
Cover me with fleece.

I Need a Home, Dad

I need a home, Dad,
Where I shall find shelter,
The warmth of a bed,
The comfort of a roof.

Should rain pour on me,
As if I have no Saviour
To pluck me from misery
And provide the four walls?

Let me have my refuge,
Where I certainly can hide
From the violence of the storm,
And the heat of that sun.

My feet are hot, bleeding.
A merciless thorn got me.
I failed to save myself
From precious protection.

The home must always be
That place of sweet rest,
Where we shall talk merrily
And swell the skies with song.

Understand Me, Dear Mum

Understand me, dear Mum.
I wasn't born for ridicule,
Norcan I dress like you
And behave like a mum.

I am a teen girl,
With wishes, dreams, and heights
To be achieved and won.
Give me that opportunity now.

Why should I behave big
When I am small and active?
Lead me to be myself,
So young, bright, and hopeful!

Shall I be a discoverer,
To explore the world unknown
And attempt feats undone?
Propel me without the knock.

Companions of My Age

Companions of my age,
Let us meet together
To beat the weather,
Free from the cage.

Friends of my time,
Are you all fine?
Come, let us dance.
It is our chance!

Players of the flute,
Blow the sweet sound;
Let the rhythm shoot.
Do not be bound.

Comrades far and near,
Cast out that fear,
Make the brave move,
That path to choose.

What is our goal?
We must now talk
As we thus walk,
Aiming for that pole.

Food Is Gone, Alas!

Food is gone, alas!
What shall we do?
Timmy, you must go
Find those precious crumbs,
Left on the table,
Where all royals feed.

Is life so unfair
That people thus flee,
Leaving us to starve,
Sipping from these tears
That paint the gloom
As it gets dark?

Next morn shall come.
What shall we expect?
We are all waiting.
See how they feel
As we shall ponder
Days gone by.

Keep Me Company, Dear Friends

Keep me company, dear friends.
Let me not wander all alone.
I dare not travel around
Without companions to share
The joys, the sorrows, the burdens.

The going up there is tough.
Jim, come up and join me,
Pull me up round the corners.
I shall not fall with you around.
Cheer me up, make me bright.

Downslope is tougher, step by step.
Let go that rope, the lifeline,
So I hold on till the end.
I shall soon come down.
Light the torch, my candlelight.

Have you heard what happened,
When Pat tried all alone
To fly across that bridge,
Without escort, without counsel,
How she missed the mark?

I must roll on below the beacon,
Take me up all steps till I reach
The rooftop once, once again,
To breathe success, and smell victory.
Thank you, my dear, for guiding me.

I Want to Be Loved

I want to be loved,
Like a little toddler
Who is ever smiling
As the going gets rough.

I want to be praised,
Patted on the back,
When I do good
And please my mentor.

I want to be led
Every step of the way.
Let me not stray,
Untended like that sheep!

I want to be smart,
Like all my peers
Who go round town,
Hunting down the pleasure.

Oh, Lord! Let Me Sing

Oh, Lord! Let me sing,
About the external King
Who rules the universe.
Please recite the verse.

I shall sing to release
That pent-up force,
As I do the course,
With so much ease.

Bring me my cup,
Overflowing with syrup.
I shall get up soon
And enjoy my life.

Let me take that cheer,
That is a real delight.
I shall wait as it clears.
Comfort is now near.

Down the Straight Lane

Down the straight lane,
I see the end,
Where life is there,
Undisturbed by any means,
Where the sun keeps shining
And never stops.

Down the straight lane,
I cherish those dreams,
Of a life of hope,
And cakes galore,
Where tears are dried,
And smiles bring cheer.

Down the straight lane,
I am never alone,
For friends come near,
To take my hand,
And lift me upwards,
To the hilltop there.

Down the straight lane,
I am never alone,
For Christ is near
Ever, always loving,
To provide that light,
I need, so dear.

Who Hears My Call?

Who hears my call?
I appeal to you all,
Who stride and stroll
Like grass so tall.

How long shall it be
Before noon arrives?
I shall search like a bee,
Which has mastered the hives.

Shall I grope in the dark,
Leaving that spotty park,
Where dreams don't die,
And stars ever shine?

I am not all alone.
Should I grab the phone
And call for rescue,
For the priceless cure?

ON HIV AND AIDS

Stop the Deadly Virus

Stop the deadly virus.
It is drawing near,
Moving fast past trees,
Burning grass all round,
Bringing terror and pain.

Who will brave the cold
To confront the enemy,
The number one foe here?
Let us break his teeth,
So he stops biting.

How deadly you are!
You plant that misery
And break up families
That wander and stray,
In the cage so frightful!

I fear HIV and AIDS.
Grant me the gloves to fight
The enemy with those daggers.
Two-edged they sit,
And lurk in the dark.

I Am Sick, Mum; Support Me

I am sick, Mum; support me.
No friend is near; they shun me.
I am cornered; friends fly away.
Is this the end of the road?

I am thin, bony skin, and done!
I dread to think, lost all hope.
Be near, Chipo, my sister.
Pass over that precious hand.

My hope is gone, gone forever!
My faith is shattered; where do I turn?
I see a star, bright, shining forth,
Coming from that hopeful east.

Whose Fault Is It?

Let me know who brought this curse,
The AIDS scourge, the frightful foe.
It may be mine, my own fault.
Does this matter? Am I not human,
Like everybody else?

Love me, talk to me, say something,
Something nice, and cheer my being!
Who is to blame for my status?
Is it my mum? Is it you, Dad?
Does it matter who?

Shall I reverse the wrongs long done?
Shall I denounce myself, my being a child,
And pretend nobody cares?
No, never, never can it be!
I shall accept, and start to rise.

Wait in Patience

Hear my appeal, all ye teens.
Avoid the sex, till time is ripe.
Time will come; do not be keen
To fall in love and go that deep.
Avoid the trouble, prevent that leap,
The step of danger, be forewarned!

Be fully clear that sex will come,
To be enjoyed in sweet wedlock.
Avoid the corners, the thorny shortcuts,
That have destroyed so many teens
In their lives' prime, gone down that drain,
Never to return to their same selves!

That disease so deadly has claimed a life,
A population of promising teens,
Who could have blossomed
And built lovely homes and towers,
To serve our nation and bring us peace.

Lonely, Lonely Am I

Lonely, lonely am I.
Father's gone, gone forever!
My star is gone, never to return.
A stranger came to snatch him away!

Lonely, lonely am I.
Mother is no more, struck by lightning!
That dreaded visitor took her away,
Never to return to offer me comfort.

Lonely, lonely am I.
Now I'm fatherless, motherless,
With kids to tend, left all alone!
Did I give birth, all these seeds?
No, no, they were abandoned without a dollar.

Lonely, lonely am I.
I need these friends to cheer me up.
I need to play and see the sun.
Shall I not grow, and reach the skies?

Is It My Fault?

Is it my fault that I am here,
Engrossed in pain like this?
All by myself, without a care.
I'll tell the world with confidence,
I shall attempt to stay alive.

I have possessed and repossessed
My heritage. I'll start to live
And be myself. I shall enjoy
What life shall offer to me at will.
I shall begin to make a move.

Where are my friends? Come, surround me.
Then let's go fishing and play the game.
Let's win and laugh, like never before.
Forget the past, forget what happened.
I shall enjoy to eat a pie.

Frightful disease, where is your bite?
I shall ignore you, get on with life.
I shall excel, as never before,
To claim my rights and lead the team.
I shall accept, and cheer the world!

My Faith

My faith shall keep me going,
Though I am sick and seem forgotten.
My Lord is near, to keep me smiling.
I long to sing and share the joy
Of being alive, to see the world.
I shall rejoice, as I believe
And trust Almighty to keep me warm,
Beneath the wings, the comfort rings.

What Caused My Sickness?

What caused my sickness?
I want to know.
Perhaps the films, uncensored true.
I fed on stories of sex so free.
No one to blame; I should have known.

What caused my problem?
Maybe those friends, who led the way,
I followed them and fell astray,
They failed to lead; I swept along!

What caused my downfall?
Could it be my mum, my own dear dad,
Who failed to lead, walk by example?
I followed timidly and saw them perish,
And here I am, without a model!

Prevention, Prevention

Prevention, prevention is better than cure.
The AIDS pandemic is sure so real,
To wipe the young, the prime of life,
To sap our hope, the pride of nations.
Who can survive without the teens?

Prevention, prevention is better than cure.
Don't feed on books, the free unlicensed.
The words that talk of nothing but sex,
To feed your brain with sensual pleasure,
That lead you nowhere but into trouble.

Prevention, prevention is better than cure.
AIDS is that killer; avoid the sting!
Be safe always, and live a life,
A choosy life, to know the wrong,
Avoid the wrong, and do the right.

I'm Dying, Mum

I'm dying, Mum; can you save me?
The star of life is gone,
Never to return!
Good-bye, dear Dad,
Your son is no more,
Gone with the wind,
Never to come back!
Good-bye world, good-bye friends.
Shall we ever meet and share the life?
My life is gone, and so beware.

OUR PROBLEMS

We Are the Teens

We are the teens.
We need to know
Who is prepared to lead the way.
We lack the leader to show to us
The bright light and star
That shines and leads, to gains untold.
We lack a model to light the candle
So we can see the light of day,
So we can walk, and run, and fly
Without the twigs, the stones, and humps.

I Am Confused

As I grow now, what I do I do?
I am confused, about myself.
Can someone tell, announce to me.
What's tickling in, inside myself?

I'm afraid, to grope and tumble,
Into the dark, inside the maze.
Who shall untangle that mess for me?
Truly, someone must answer.

As I discover the world around,
Do I understand what's going on?
I long to know, to just discover,
What is in store, in store for me.

A Girl Calls

I'm Suzy of 6 Denver Avenue,
Once I was young, a kid indeed,
But now I know I'm no longer small.
I've since become that big, big girl
Around the street, a full-blown blonde.

I have a feeling; I feel uneasy.
I grow so big, the boys are talking.
They say I'm round,
Ready for kisses, and hugs, and love.

Shall I respond? If so, just how?
Noone told me the time would come
For me to bloom.
What do I do? Whom shall I call?

I Am a Boy

I am a boy, or is it true?
I think not so; I must have changed.
Who will tell me what has become
Of me of late? I do not know.

I can no longer play with mud, with sticks.
I must have grown.
Am I a man, or what am I?
I look around. For sure, I've changed!

I look around; I see the girls.
That girl next door, oh, she's so pretty!
Yet something in me keeps ticking on.
Noone called me to forewarn me
That I shall grow, and be the real me.

As Teens Look Round

As teens look round, so wide awake,
They see the world, the life so new.
They see the change, and want to know.
They question adults, who just keep mum.
The silence is so unnerving
To all the youths as they demand
To know their world,
And so discover how to navigate,
To learn and cherish, discard and conquer.

Let Me Discover

Let me discover the mind around.
Why does my dad refuse to answer?
I ask him questions; he tells me that
It's all taboo, don't ask too much!

Is there a boundary of what to ask?
Is there a stop to what I should know?
Mum must come out, out in the open.
I'm scared to ask, to know myself.

Shall I rebel and go away,
Away from home, and seek the answer
About the world that surrounds me?
I need the answers, to all my queries.

The Young Criminal

The teen without direction,
The boy who is rejected,
And the girl without a comforter.
What will happen?

The answers are not forthcoming.
The boy is leaderless and
The girl lacks a role model.
What will happen?

Answers must be found,
Somewhat devious though they might be.
The young mind turns criminal,
Becomes deviant.

Is there a rescue package?
Is it the boy's fault?
Is it the girl's fault?
Whose fault is it, then?

Parents, Nurture Your Children

Parents, nurture your children.
Do not let them wander,
Else they get whisked away,
Blown by the wind.

Take time to teach,
To walk and talk,
Else they get snatched away
By the tormenter, without whim.

Parents, laugh and joke,
Enjoy the company of your children.
Let them share with you,
Else they get swept by the current.

Parents, do you really care?
Have you discovered your nestlings
And known who they are?
Parents, do you really care?

Have you discovered your sucklings,
And known who they are?
Else they get broken, never to be
Their same selves, same again.

Question Concerning God

I have a question to ask:
Where did I come from?
How did I exist, and by whom?
These questions bother me.

Someone knocked one day
At my doorstep and explained,
Took time to introduce the Saviour,
Who sacrificed His life for me.

Now I know myself,
That I have a relationship,
A long-lasting friendship,
That the Saviour lives,
Guides me all the way.

Time to Crave, Time to Achieve

Youth is the time,
The time to crave,
The time to achieve.
I shall succeed and compete.

Shall I not be counted,
Be known by my friends,
That I am better,
Worthy, and towering high?

Yes, the time has come.
Success knocks at the door.
I shall open and embrace.
I shall enjoy myself.

OUR VIEWS

Do Not Taunt Me

Do not taunt me.
I am always right.
Why bother about my movements?
Please mind your business,
And I shall mind mine.

Do not tell me what to do.
I know it all.
I have my answers.
Why bother me at all,
Whether I'm right or wrong?

Do not tell me who to play with.
I have got my friends;
They are neither wrong nor right.
They are friends,
And I enjoy their company.

Do not tell me where to go.
Don't order me when to come back.
I shall find my way.
I am on, on top of the world!

I Can Never Be You

I can never be you, Mum.
I'm young and vibrant.
Your rules I don't need.
I'll have it my way.

Follow me, Mum.
Let's go for the fashion.
We are the teens;
We know it all.

We live in our own,
Our own world.
Let me enjoy,
Enjoy my space.

I Choose to Wander Alone

I choose to wander alone
With myself, uplift my ego.
Leave me alone. Don't shout.
I choose my way, not yours.

I choose to sit, enjoy the sun.
I choose to sleep and be at peace,
To wake up when I choose,
So what do I care?

I choose to shout, till the roof is split!
To clear my voice, elevate myself,
I choose to sing, tuneful, tuneless,
Without any drums to keep me company.

I choose to walk, facing south.
You choose to go, facing north.
What does it matter, where I face?
Let me enjoy my will, my company.

The Teens Are Here

We are here, we are there,
We are nowhere, we are somewhere.
Take time to watch, and to smile,
Smile always. Don't frown.
We make the world
And turn the globe.

I Come Home, There Is No Mum

I come home, there is no Mum.
I sit there, no food to eat.
I lie there, waiting for Dad,
Who chooses to come at break of day.

I pace around to see the brother;
Noone comes upfront.
I gaze awide; no sister comes,
No smile, no song.

I go, go out,
Out there I see
A gang of four.
We walk together, in unison.

Let's go away, beyond.
There is no home,
No tea to drink,
No air to breathe.

Hey, Boy, Stop There

"Hey, boy, stop there!"
I look up, I look aside.
"Hey, lanky, stop!"
Who do I see?
Mr. Policeman with handcuffs.

Am I a thief? Am I a robber?
"You sniffed the glue,
We'll sort you out!"
No! No! No, sir!
Let me explain.
In that packet I saw cigars.

Stop taunting me.
Look at yourself.
Take out that stick,
Right in your eye!

Hop, Step, Jump

Hop, step, jump.
Where do I go?
If I go up, I see the blue.
Nothing to touch,
Nothing to feel.

Hop, step, jump.
I look beneath.
There, in the dark,
I hear the bones
Calling my name.

Hop, step, jump.
I look ahead,
I see the boys.
They welcome me
Into the cave.

Detective Inspector Hangman

Detective Inspector Hangman
Went to the shop to buy bread.
He met the girls stealing the cups,
He saw the girls eating the pie.

"Hey, girls! Stop! Thief!
You are under house arrest.
You shall regret
What you have done!"

"We have no house,"
Answered the girls.
"We abide here,
This rightful home."

Friend of the Teens

Friend of the teens, hear our cry.
Comforter, be near us
As we pray, as we plead.
We are forgotten, cast away.
Lead us to peace, to waters still!
Show us the light, bright morning star.
Hold our hands firm, right in the grip
Of that Love, eternal care.

Show Me Myself

Show me myself,
Where I belong,
So that I may long
To be that self.

Supply my needs.
Pluck away the weeds
That haunt my way,
As I see the day.

Keep me company, dear.
Always be near
To behold my need,
Even as you heed.

When at last I rest,
Cosy in that nest,
Let me face the challenge
I can easily manage.

Review Requested:

If you loved this book, would you please provide a review at Amazon.com?

CPSIA information can be obtained
at www.ICGtesting.com
Printed in the USA
LVHW090504020420
652001LV00001B/38